GOD'S HEART FOR YOU

100 Day Devotional

Uta Milewski is one of the most genuine followers of Jesus I know. Her writing skills are greatly enhanced by her ability to hear from God and write it down. I have read many devotionals and when I read *God's Heart for You* I often think, "This is exactly what I needed to hear today." Her personal thoughts and practical wisdom from the Holy Spirit will enlighten and inspire you. This will become one of your favorite devotionals. You will want to buy one for a friend.

Dr. Ronald V. Burgio
Lead Pastor, Love Joy Church
President, Elim Fellowship

These heartfelt devotional thoughts will be an encouragement to all who read them. Uta has long been a blessing to her local church, and I'm glad to see her stepping out to bless even more in the Body of Christ.

Dr Robert Stearns
Eagles' Wings Ministries

In *God's Heart for You*, Uta Milewski transparently admits that her ability to hear God was developed during a period of self-doubt and uncertainty. But this devotional is more than Uta's story. She wants to take you, the reader, on a journey to train your ear to hear His voice above the noise. God is still speaking. Will you learn to hear His voice?

Rev. Al Warner
Director, Set Free Inc.

GOD'S HEART FOR YOU

100 Day Devotional

Uta Milewski

Foreword by Dr. Mark Virkler
Communion with God Ministries

LoveJoy PUBLISHING

God's Heart for You
Copyright © 2012 by Uta P. Milewski

Third Edition
Published by Love Joy Publishing
5423 Genesee Street
Lancaster, NY 14086
www.lovejoy.org

ISBN: 978-0-9820062-1-4

Cover Design: Paula Bordin

Printed in the United States of America

Acknowledgements

I thank God for the staff and people of Love Joy Church who've been my friends and my family for so many years.

Thanks to my husband, Bob, for being so faithful and hardworking, for keeping our household grounded and orderly and giving me the freedom and encouragement to pursue my dreams. God knew what He was doing when He had you find me on the door stoop 37 years ago. Too few people know what you've sacrificed to have your wife so involved in church ministry.

Thank you to my boss, pastor, coach and friend, Dr. Ron Burgio, for pushing me beyond my comfort zone and encouraging me to put my dreams into action. You make every day exciting.

Dr. Mark Virkler, thank you for teaching me to hear God's voice.

And thanks to Roger Kerl for catching my reference errors in the first edition.

Foreword

"My Sheep Hear My Voice..." (Jn. 10:27)

Jesus said it! Uta demonstrates it! You can do it!

Many years ago, I read the book God Calling by Two Listeners. It was a book of journaling, just like Uta's. I was so amazed that people could hear God's voice and write it down. It seemed like an impossibility to me. What amazing people these "two listeners" must have been. How I hungered to have this experience.

Now, we have the privilege of training others how to hear God's voice. Uta's book is a wonderful demonstration that God is still speaking today. After 500 years of the Church believing there is no living contact between God and man, this wall of separation is being broken down. The Wonderful Counselor is speaking words of healing into our hearts. This book is a demonstration of that fact and His loving words provide healing, inspiration and life!

So enjoy these 100 daily devotionals, and let them call you into doing the same thing that Uta has done. Learn how to hear His voice, so you can receive His words of life into your own heart on a daily basis. He is no respecter of people. Jesus is speaking to you, just as he has spoken to Uta. Let His fresh daily words spill down over your life, cleansing you, healing you and restoring you.

Uta, thank you for your faithfulness in pursuing a life lived by the Spirit. Thank you for demonstrating in print that God STILL speaks today. Thank you for sharing your innermost heart with us, allowing the blessings you have received to spill over onto us.

Enjoy the words of the Lord.

Mark Virkler
Author of *4 Keys to Hearing God's Voice*
www.cwgministries.org

Introduction

Do you sometimes struggle with thoughts and feelings that you don't measure up? I do and I sometimes need a second opinion and a different perspective.

In 2006, during an intense season of first doubt and then searching, God gave me His opinion, His heart for me. It set in motion the victories and freedom I now experience in life.

I pray you'll be encouraged by the Scriptures and thoughts God gave me during that time.

Blessings,
Uta

Light

This is the message He has given us to announce to you: God is light and there is no darkness in Him at all.
1 John 1:5 NAS

Light without darkness, oh how it energizes your soul. When you let Me in, and allow Me to bring that light into your being, it brings clarity, joy, love, wisdom, refreshing, and energy. All that is of Me is available to you if you open your heart to My light.

Every good gift and every perfect gift is from above, and comes down from the Father of lights, with whom there is no variation or shadow of turning.
James 1:17

Nothing eclipses the light of My presence. If you abandon yourself to Me, if you cast every care on Me, if you hold no areas of your life back, then as My light penetrates, it searches and cleanses your heart.

Day 2

Faith, Hope & Love

My love for you is great. I know you. And I love you. You wonder how I can love you if I know you so well. I know you better than you know yourself. I know that you were made for glory. I know that you were made in the image of God. I know that you were made for eternity. You are a child of the king, temporarily displaced from the palace. Heaven with all its glories is your home.

...now for a little while, if necessary,
you have been grieved by various trials,
so that the tested genuineness of your faith--
more precious than gold that perishes though it is
tested by fire-- may be found to result in praise and
glory and honor at the revelation of Jesus Christ.
1 Peter 1:6-7 ESV

Your trials and tests come to refine you. I desire that you have faith, hope and love, and I will remove from you all fear, doubt and anger.

Fasting

Fasting creates the illusion of weakness. It presents a face of poverty in order to draw in those forces that feed on poverty. It is a tactic to force a confrontation with the demonic in a seemingly weak person, for Satan goes after the weak and the hungry, but when you are weak then you are strong. Purposeful fasting draws Satan into an ambush. It is a tactic of war. Those who fast for war rely on Me. Don't make a big deal out of fasting, for it relies on secrecy to work. You are under cover, standing in the gap for the weak, drawing off the forces that would otherwise attack them. But you will be victorious, for your weakness is your strength. You will not give in to the temptation presented to you. Your strength is not in riches and in being well fed physically. Your strength lies in being well fed spiritually. The victory you gain will be yours forever.

Day 4

Help them!

But you have not honored the God who gives you the breath of life and controls your destiny!
Daniel 5:23b NLT

Many live ignorant of Me. They neither honor Me nor thank Me, but I still control their destiny. How blessed are those who know Me, who know My love and My plans for them. I want no one to perish in their ignorance. I want all to know the way to Me, to eternal life, to the joy of Our presence.

Help them! Help them! Help them!

For I know the plans I have for you," declares the LORD,
"plans to prosper you and not to harm you,
plans to give you hope and a future."
Jeremiah 29:11 NIV

Harvest

Then Jesus came to them and said, "All authority in heaven and on earth has been given to Me. Therefore go and make disciples of all nations, baptizing them in the name of the Father and of the Son and of the Holy Spirit, and teaching them to obey everything I have commanded you. And surely I am with you always, to the very end of the age." Matthew 28:18-20 NIV

I am the Lord of the harvest. As you have followed Me in obedience into the throne room of grace, so make the shift now and follow Me into the harvest. Who will go for us? Many of My children want to go, but lack the awareness of My authority on earth. You already know My authority in heaven over all principalities and powers. Cry out to Me for the awareness of My authority on earth. You have identified with My humility, now identify with My authority.

The earth is the LORD's, and all its fullness, the world and those who dwell therein. Psalm 24:1

Day 6

Firm

Forever, O Lord, your word stands firm in heaven.
Your faithfulness extends to every generation.
Psalm 119:89-90 NLT

It is almost impossible for you to grasp how firm My word stands. If I didn't allow you to experience My faithfulness through your trials, you would hardly know it. I speak no idle words. Everything I speak is established, created and unshakable. I welcome you to abide in My word, to make My word your home. Nothing is more real. Trust in My word. I am the word and I am truth, so trust in Me. I offer you My Spirit to help you cling to My truth.

Now this is eternal life:
that they may know you,
the only true God, and Jesus Christ,
whom you have sent.
John 17:3 NIV

Follow Me

Follow Me, and I will make you fishers of men. I will make you. You don't have to be afraid that you can't do what I ask you to do. I will make you. I will help you. Just come along with Me. Just serve Me with the talent you have, I will add things to your life that were not there before. Didn't Peter show you? On his own he was more apt to turn people away from Me, but I made him into a fisher of men. I caused My Spirit to rest on him and speak through him. Just be humble and serve Me. Just be eager to receive everything I have for you. You have not yet tapped into all the power available to you. There's no reason for you to lack confidence.

Now to Him who is able to do far more abundantly than all that we ask or think, according to the power at work within us, to Him be glory in the church and in Christ Jesus
throughout all generations, forever and ever. Amen.
Ephesians 3:20-21 ESV

Day 8

Fear of the Lord

I am a friend to anyone who fears you--anyone who obeys your commandments. Psalm 119:63 NLT

You are becoming acquainted with the fear of the Lord.

The fear of the LORD is to hate evil; pride and arrogance and the evil way and the perverse mouth I hate. Proverbs 8:13 NAS

Yes, you can sense it even in your own heart, the fear that causes you to shrink away from pride and arrogance and evil. It is very real now. I am pouring it out on the earth. It is a part of My glory that will cover the earth. You desire to know all of Me? This is a part of Me that I have held back in intensity until this time. It is My grieving heart over My children. I grieve over My children when they fail to acknowledge My love and care for them. There is great power in My grief.

The Spirit of the LORD shall rest upon Him, The Spirit of wisdom and understanding, The Spirit of counsel and might, The Spirit of knowledge and of the fear of the LORD. His delight is in the fear of the LORD, And He shall not judge by the sight of His eyes, Nor decide by the hearing of His ears; Isaiah 11:2-3

Nothing

I will no longer talk much with you,
for the ruler of this world is coming,
and he has nothing in Me.
John 14:30

I want the ruler of this world to have nothing in you, as he had nothing in Me. Holiness is like a smooth wall without footholds, but when you allow sin in your life, you create footholds on which the ruler of this world scales your walls and conquers you. Sin gives him power and a claim over you. When I forgive your sin, those footholds are removed. So don't hold onto anything you know is evil, because I don't want you to have anything in common with evil. I want joy for you. My rules are not to make you miserable, but to keep you from misery. I don't want My arch enemy to have power over you.

...just as he who called you is holy, so be holy in all
you do; for it is written: "Be holy, because I am
holy."
1 Peter 1:15-16 NIV

Day 10

Inheritance

Blessed be the God and Father of our Lord Jesus Christ! According to his great mercy, he has caused us to be born again to a living hope through the resurrection of Jesus Christ from the dead, to an inheritance that is imperishable, undefiled, and unfading, kept in heaven for you, who by God's power are being guarded through faith for a salvation ready to be revealed in the last time.
1 Peter 1:3-5 ESV

Heaven holds your inheritance. Your reward is with Me. I rejoice in your trust and love in Me, for that is what secures your inheritance and reward.

Though you have not seen Him, you love Him. Though you do not now see Him, you believe in Him and rejoice with joy that is inexpressible and filled with glory, obtaining the outcome of your faith, the salvation of your souls. 1 Peter 1:8-9 ESV

Absolute holiness

And this is the basic law of the Temple: absolute holiness! Ezekiel 43:12 NLT

I bring absolute holiness into your heart. Your heart is My temple. I will help you and never give up on you. You are made in My image and you were designed to carry My glory in your heart. I have redeemed you and I cleanse you so that My presence and glory can reside in you. Let not your heart be delighted in anything but My presence. Be careful when you find yourself focusing on your accomplishments, on riches or on people, whether in a positive or a negative way. Seek first My kingdom and My righteousness and all these other things will be added to you. You will have other joys, but don't put them first. Let them be added to you at the perimeter, in the outer court of your heart. Absolute holiness means your heart is set apart for Me with no other idols of delight.

Suddenly, the glory of the God of Israel appeared from the east. The sound of his coming was like the roar of rushing waters, and the whole landscape shone with his glory... And the glory of the Lord came into the Temple through the east gateway.
Ezekiel 43:2, 4 NLT

Day 12

Gates

Open for me the gates where the righteous enter,
and I will go in and thank the LORD. Those gates
lead to the presence of the LORD, and the godly
enter there.
Psalm 118:19-20 NLT

Come, come through the gates. Come into My
presence for I love you, and I want to see you and
let My face shine upon you. Yes I see you always,
but you don't always see Me. Turn to Me. Turn to
My presence so I can fill you with light and love and
joy. Open your heart to My love, the love that is
stronger than death; the love that is stronger than
sin. Please see that you are made for purity and
holiness. Please see that sin is beneath you. Come
up higher. Come away and let My glory sanctify
your temple.

And there I will meet with the children of Israel,
and the tabernacle shall be sanctified by My glory.
Exodus 29:43 KJV

Fresh Water

Does a spring of water bubble out with both fresh water and bitter water...? No, and you can't draw fresh water from a salty pool. James 3:11a, 12 NLT

I would have you bubble out with fresh water. I would have you speak blessing and not cursing. Speak about yourself and others what you hear Me say. Don't describe the condition, but speak the potential. Let Me bubble out from within you when you speak. My Spirit is always pure and fresh. My wisdom is from above.

But the wisdom that is from above is first pure, then peaceable, gentle, willing to yield, full of mercy and good fruits, without partiality and without hypocrisy. James 3:17

Day 14

Glory

Whoever believes in Me, as the Scripture has said,
'Out of his heart will flow rivers of living water.'
John 7:38 ESV

For God, who said, "Let light shine out of darkness,"
has shone in our hearts to give the light of the
knowledge of the glory of God in the face of Jesus
Christ.
2 Corinthians 4:6 ESV

For the earth will be filled with the knowledge of the
glory of the LORD as the waters cover the sea.
Habakkuk 2:14 ESV

Do you understand that My glory flows through you?
Do you understand that the earth will be filled with
the knowledge of My glory as you, My children,
allow Me to flow through you? It is not just in word
that I flow, but in power. My glory flows from you to
fill the earth. I want your hearts to be open without
any obstruction so I can use you. Don't be
concerned with what you should say or do with My
anointing. Just let Me flow from you into the earth,
saturating the soil.

Presence

Gentle creek   Niagara Falls   Floodgates

And so I walk in the Lord's presence as I live here on earth!
Psalm 116:9 NLV

I am near. I am available. As you walk in My presence, you bring My presence wherever you go, and as you call on Me, I will manifest.

Each of My children manifests who I am in a unique way. Each of you uses in this earth the various gifts I have given you, but it is all of the same Spirit.

Some represent Me as a gentle creek. Others show Me off in power like Niagara Falls. Still others bring forth the things of God like open floodgates.

It is all pleasing to Me.

Day 16

Altar

We have an altar
from which the priests in the temple on earth
have no right to eat.
Hebrews 13:10 NLT

Do you understand what this means? The priests in the temple were allowed to eat from the altar. They were permitted to partake of the sacrifice that had been offered to God. This is what sustained them. You have a different altar, the one where I am the sacrifice offered to God. When you take communion, when you partake of Me, when you take Me into yourself, when you eat of My flesh and drink of My blood, you eat from this altar. This is very necessary to nurture you and to sustain you. You cannot lead an overcoming life without it. Yes, I want you to do this in a real physical sense by sharing the bread and the wine among your brothers and sisters. I also want you to do it in the Spirit by receiving from Me the nurture and joy I want to give you. Receive now.

Shaking

When God spoke from Mount Sinai his voice shook the earth, but now he makes another promise: "Once again I will shake not only the earth but the heavens also." This means that the things on earth will be shaken, so that only eternal things will be left. Since we are receiving a kingdom that cannot be destroyed, let us be thankful and please God by worshipping him with holy fear and awe. For our God is a consuming fire.
Hebrews 12:26-29 NLT

When I spoke from Mount Sinai, My presence was unmistakable. The people knew I spoke and they feared Me. Yet they did not obey Me. Now when I speak in a still, small voice those who desire Me are eager to obey Me. Those who hunger and thirst for righteousness can hear Me and the pure will see Me. I have always longed to dwell among My people and I long for it still. When I shake the heavens and the earth, cling to the Rock.

Day 18

Discipline

God's discipline is always good for us, so that we might share in his holiness. No discipline is enjoyable while it is happening—it's painful! But afterward there will be a peaceful harvest of right living for those who are trained in this way.
Hebrews 12:10b, 11 NLT

Each day you have a choice. Each day you face a fork in the road. If you listen to My voice, I will guide you, but if you make a wrong step I will correct you. Is this not because I love you? You have a choice each day: to walk the ancient path of obedience by grace or to veer off into one of two detours. These detours are either the way of self and flesh or the opposite way of legalism and judgment. I would have you stay on the center path of obedience by grace. This is where I walk and where you will find My presence. Anything else leads to destruction. You want to share in My holiness? Then walk with Me on the highway of holiness.

Ancient Highway

Ponder the path of your feet, and let all your ways be established. Do not turn to the right or the left; remove your foot from evil.
Proverbs 4:26-27

A highway shall be there, and a road, and it shall be called the Highway of Holiness. The unclean shall not pass over it, but it shall be for others. Whoever walks the road, although a fool, shall not go astray.
Isaiah 35:8

This is what the LORD says: "Stand at the crossroads and look; ask for the ancient paths, ask where the good way is, and walk in it, and you will find rest for your souls... Jeremiah 6:16 NIV

[My people] have caused themselves to stumble in their ways [broad, trodden roads], from the ancient paths, to walk in pathways [byways] and not on a highway [mounted up, exalted road.]
Jeremiah 18:15

Day 20

Peace

Yes, I speak peace to your busy mind. Don't let your thoughts scramble around like a hamster on a wheel. Let Me lift you up to the path with Me. Let's walk forward in peace. Trust Me with all your heart and don't lean on your own understanding. That means, don't try to figure out all the complexities of life, but hold onto My hand and trust Me to lead you. Come away from the paths of anger, fear and judgment and step up onto the path of faith, hope and love. This will always be My path for you. No matter what happens in the world, your path will be paved with faith, hope and love.

And let the peace of God rule in your hearts, to which also you were called in one body; and be thankful. Let the word of Christ dwell in you richly in all wisdom, teaching and admonishing one another in psalms and hymns and spiritual songs, singing with grace in your hearts to the Lord. And whatever you do in word or deed, do all in the name of the Lord Jesus, giving thanks to God the Father through Him.
Colossians 3:15-17

Narrow

Enter by the narrow gate. For the gate is wide and the way is easy that leads to destruction, and those who enter by it are many.
Matthew 7:13 ESV

When you step through the narrow gate into My Kingdom, your life expands. You become not just an expression of the form this world molds you into, but an expression of the vastness of My glory. Your life becomes an expression of My heart. Space is unending and time is eternal, and when you belong to Me, you need to fear neither. I am master of both. Step beyond the explainable, the measurable existence of this world and enter into the realm of My love. I am the way, and the truth, and the life. No one comes to the Father except through Me.

And may you have the power to understand, as all God's people should, how wide, how long, how high, and how deep his love is. May you experience the love of Christ, though it is too great to understand fully. Then you will be made complete with all the fullness of life and power that comes from God.
Ephesians 3:18-19 NLT

Day 22

Downcast?

Why are you downcast, O my soul? Why so disturbed within me? Put your hope in God, for I will yet praise him, my Savior and my God.
Psalm 42:5 NIV

When you are downcast, it shows where your focus has been. Isn't it true? When you are downcast, you can be sure that you have been meditating on what's wrong in you and in the world, and not on what's right with Me. Come on, lift your eyes. You are in this world, but not of it. Blessed are those who mourn, for they will be comforted. You've mourned the wrong, now let Me comfort you. Cast all your cares on Me, because I care for you. Release your anxieties to Me - Each one. I have already suffered on the cross for these things. Yes they grieve Me, but I knew about them, and I have already atoned for them. The weight of the sin of the world has already crushed Me. So come with Me, see Me bearing the sins of the world, see Me dead and buried, but don't stop there. Come on, see Me raised again. See Me raised to honor, the honor of one who was willing to stoop down to the lowest point, yet was raised up to the highest. You are with Me. Just know that blessed are those who hunger and thirst for righteousness, for they shall be satisfied. Lift your eyes to Me in that hope.

Will

I am pleased when you wait for My direction. When you say, "not my will but Your will," really wait for My will to be revealed to you. Don't have your mind all made up about your plans and then ask Me for My will. No matter what happens in the world, I will propel you into the future I have planned for you, if you let Me.

Remember the former things of old, for I am God, and there is no other; I am God, and there is none like Me, Declaring the end from the beginning, and from ancient times things that are not yet done, saying, 'My counsel shall stand, and I will do all My pleasure,' Calling a bird of prey from the east, the man who executes My counsel, from a far country. Indeed I have spoken it; I will also bring it to pass. I have purposed it; I will also do it.
Isaiah 46:9-11 ESV

Day 24

Pliable

Stay pliable in My hands. I lead you each day by many small adjustments with My still small voice. The greatest hindrances in your life are the areas that are hardened. Don't keep areas of your life aside where you refuse My adjustments. Don't be afraid of My correction and don't be protective. Your own power to protect is not greater than mine. I do not shame you or blame you, but in all things I long to lead you in paths of righteousness for My name's sake. Don't even be protective of your reputation or how you appear to people, but be genuine from the heart, like a child.

Then He said, "Go out, and stand on the mountain before the LORD." And behold, the LORD passed by, and a great and strong wind tore into the mountains and broke the rocks in pieces before the LORD, but the LORD was not in the wind; and after the wind an earthquake, but the LORD was not in the earthquake; and after the earthquake a fire, but the LORD was not in the fire; and after the fire a still small voice.
1 King 19:11-12

Fresh Fountain

There is a fresh fountain within you. Though you may have grief and hurts, temptations and anger, the fountain within you cleanses you and brings you fresh hope that I am at work. The work I do in the world does not always look or feel pleasant, but it always is beneficial for My children. How often have you prayed, "Thy kingdom come, Thy will be done on earth as it is in heaven." When I answer that prayer, it may be to the detriment of earthly kings and kingdoms. When My kingdom comes and My will is done, another kingdom and another will must yield. It involves conflict. Don't be confused by that conflict. If a kingdom or will does not yield, it becomes even more perverted and the wrath for that one is multiplied. Yet there is still a little time to yield.

"If anyone thirsts, let him come to Me and drink. He who believes in Me, as the Scripture has said, out of his heart will flow rivers of living water."
John 7:37b-38

Day 26

Without ceasing

We have a High Priest who sat down in the place of honor beside the throne of the majestic God in heaven. There he ministers in the heavenly Tabernacle, the true place of worship that was built by the Lord and not by human hands.
Hebrews 8:1b-2 NLT

You have access to this true place of worship. You can come here at any time. This is your home and the home of My Spirit that lives in you. My glory and My presence are here all the time, ministering, interceding for you and worshipping the Father. When you enter into the kind of worship the Father seeks in Spirit and in truth, you come here. I long for you always to be here, even while you are working or reading or talking to your friends. Let the spirit part of you stay in touch with Me. That's how you pray without ceasing. That's how you stay on the highway of holiness and remain obedient to My leading. **I will put My laws in your mind so you will understand them, and I will engrave them on your heart so you will obey them.**

Strong Tower

For there is one God and one Mediator between God and men, the Man Christ Jesus, who gave Himself a ransom for all, to be testified in due time.
1 Timothy 2:5-6

For we do not have a High Priest who cannot sympathize with our weaknesses, but was in all points tempted as we are, yet without sin.
Hebrews 4:15

For it was indeed fitting that we should have such a high priest, holy, innocent, unstained, separated from sinners, and exalted above the heavens.
Hebrews 7:26 ESV

Come to Me. Come to the rock. Let nothing separate you from My love. Have no other focus, but look to Me. Your soul is anchored in the Holy of Holies, where I live to intercede to the Father on your behalf.

Peace I leave with you, My peace I give to you; not as the world gives do I give to you. Let not your heart be troubled, neither let it be afraid.
John 14:27

When all else is shaken to the core, I am not moved. My name is a strong tower.

Day 28

Endure

And because lawlessness will abound, the love of many will grow cold. But he who endures to the end shall be saved. And this gospel of the kingdom will be preached in all the world as a witness to all the nations, and then the end will come.
Matthew 24:12-14

How can you tell if your love is growing cold? If you love Me, you will obey Me. If you begin to disobey Me, you know that your love is growing cold. When you disobey Me, you will hurt others and make them sad. Endure. I give you the grace to endure as long as you walk on the highway of holiness with Me. Don't stray from the center of the highway now. Don't go peeking over the edge to see what's beyond. Don't ignore My rebuke when you leave My side. Walk with Me in grace and obedience. Hear both My "yes" and My "no." Let Me lead you with My rod and My staff.

The LORD is my shepherd; I shall not want. He makes me lie down in green pastures. He leads me beside still waters. He restores my soul. He leads me in paths of righteousness for his name's sake. Even though I walk through the valley of the shadow of death, I will fear no evil, for you are with me; your rod and your staff, they comfort me.
Psalm 23:1-4

Seeking joy

Your seeking after Me for joy is not the same as self-indulgence. You are not the originator of the desire for My joy, I am. David said of Me:

You will show me the path of life; In Your presence is fullness of joy; At Your right hand are pleasures forevermore.
Psalm 16:11

Yes, I have purpose and zeal and a desire to move in the earth by My Spirit. Yes there is a lot for you to do, but first receive the fullness of My joy. My joy gives you strength and lightens your burden. My joy is not the reward for your hard work, but the fuel that makes your work easier. My joy is your power tool. Without it, all is manual labor. With it, you'll accomplish much more in a shorter amount of time. Forge ahead in My joy. Yes, see yourself forging ahead. The more joy, the more power. The more power, the greater the conquest.

For what is our hope, or joy, or crown of rejoicing? Is it not even you in the presence of our Lord Jesus Christ at His coming?
1 Thessalonians 2:19

Day 30

Wisdom

Wisdom cries aloud in the street, in the markets she raises her voice; at the head of the noisy streets she cries out; at the entrance of the city gates she speaks: "How long, O simple ones, will you love being simple? How long will scoffers delight in their scoffing and fools hate knowledge? If you turn at My reproof, behold, I will pour out My spirit to you; I will make My words known to you. For the simple are killed by their turning away, and the complacency of fools destroys them; but whoever listens to me will dwell secure and will be at ease, without dread of disaster." Proverbs 1:20- 23; 32-33 ESV

I am releasing My wisdom into the streets, the markets, the gathering places and into places of government. I am sending out a call. Many who have never before heard it will hear it now. Who are the simple? Those who live on the surface, who have no depth of understanding, who have not yet opened their lives to My reality. I am sending out My reproof, a call to listen to the good news of the Kingdom of God. My witnesses, those who understand and carry My presence, will go out and release My wisdom into the streets.

Transparent

For the word of God is living and powerful, and sharper than any two-edged sword, piercing even to the division of soul and spirit, and of joints and marrow, and is a discerner of the thoughts and intents of the heart. And there is no creature hidden from His sight, but all things are naked and open to the eyes of Him to whom we must give account. Hebrews 4:12-13

You can be transparent before people when you have already given an account of all things before Me. I am the Word of God. When you daily expose yourself to the Word of God, both to the written Word and to the words I speak to you when you come into My presence, I thoroughly examine and sanctify you. I forgive your sins and I free you from the power of sin. I expose your weaknesses, not to cause you shame, but to let you and others see that the power is not in you, but that My grace is sufficient for you. You can boast in your weaknesses, laugh about them and be joyful, lighthearted and happy, because they are so little in My eyes. Pride and sin are heavy burdens, but weaknesses are not.

Day 32

Exceeding joy

Today, if you hear his voice, do not harden your hearts as in the rebellion, on the day of testing in the wilderness.
Hebrews 3:7-9 NIV

If you listen, you will hear My voice. And if you hear My voice, do not harden your heart. Do not lean on your own understanding. I have told you My yoke is easy and My burden is light, so don't harden you heart if I tell you a light and easy thing to do. Don't be as Naaman who expected that I would make it difficult for him to be healed. If I ask of you to sit at My feet, don't I come to you and bless you and fill you with My glory? Don't be religious and expect Me to only ask hard things of you. I am not the God of drudgery. I am the God of exceeding joy.

Then I will go to the altar of God, to God my exceeding joy...
Psalm 43:4a

I know you

I know you, like you know a favorite book. Only, you forget the details. I never forget. I know you, I have read you and I have memorized you. For I live inside of you. I am there every moment. My hand upholds you every minute of the day and night. You and I are writing the book of your life together. You are not yet finished. I know what I would like to write into your life and if you listen to My voice and obey, the chapter on your life on earth will end the way I want it to end. That chapter is only the introduction to the book. It's how you came to be the being that will live in eternity. Wait on Me daily and listen for My still small voice throughout every day. I am the author and the finisher of your faith. As I write faith into your life, and as you follow Me, you will move mountains and calm seas and do signs and wonders in My name. I am also the illustrator of your book. See the pictures and illustrations I draw. These too are of faith. When I show you one of My illustrations, have the faith for it and go after it.

Day 34

You don't know

You don't know you, and you don't fully understand how much I love you. You hope that I do. You want to know better. That's good. I have been teaching you for many years to receive My love, remember? Do you feel that little bit of tightness in your heart right now? That's where you are having a hard time receiving My love. Do you want Me to remove that? All right, I set you free of that insecurity and lie right now. Renounce it. Very good.

My desire for you is to have you in My heart. To embrace all that you are, body, soul and spirit; to wrap you in My arms and treasure you. A mother treasures her love for a baby in her heart and nothing can stop that love. Well, nothing can stop My love for you. Receive it and receive with it all I want to bless you with: wisdom, courage, friendship and joy.

All right, let it flow into you now. I am removing the stony heart and I give you a heart of flesh. My love flow will work on you. Don't worry if you can't receive it all right now. I will soften your heart continually.

Clay pot

Do you treasure the unseen, inner life? I have put eternity in your heart. It's not at the surface but in your heart. My Spirit lives and moves and strengthens you from within. I know your desire is to shine My light in the darkness, and as you obey My voice, you come out from underneath the bushel that has hidden you. My vibrant life within you will shine forth. Don't be afraid. Let the light pulse out. Let My glory shine around you. My life is in you as the torch that was in Gideon's clay pot. Why do you think the apostles were overjoyed for being counted worthy of suffering disgrace for My name? Because persecution smashes the clay pot. So don't ever be afraid of it.

And he [Gideon] divided the 300 men into three companies and put trumpets into the hands of all of them and empty jars, with torches inside the jars…
Then the three companies blew the trumpets and broke the jars.
Judges 7:16,20a ESV

Day 36

Press in

Press in. Press in. When you can't seem to find My presence, press in. Don't give up. Open your heart and draw on Me. Pull on Me. Reach for the hem of My garment. Pursue Me and you will find Me. Cry out to Me, like blind Bartimaeus did. Run after Me, because I want you to keep moving with Me. Didn't I say, "Follow Me." I'm not standing still, so keep moving along with Me. At those times when you can't seem to catch Me, you make the greatest progress. Just don't get frustrated in your pursuit. You will catch up. It pleases Me that you want to be near Me. Getting to the place where I want you is hard work. Don't give up. Press in. Press in.

And many rebuked him [Bartimaeus], telling him to be silent. But he cried out all the more, "Son of David, have mercy on me!"
Mark 10:48 ESV

Outpouring

The people of Nineveh believed God's message...
Jonah 3:5

And yes, I say, the people of Buffalo will believe God's message. I am pouring out a new measure of faith. I am coming with a new measure of My Spirit...

...the Spirit of wisdom and understanding, the Spirit of counsel and might, the Spirit of knowledge and the fear of the Lord.
Isaiah 11:2b NLT

I have shown you that I possess the Spirit without measure, without limit. So this new pouring out is without limit. It starts in one place, but it will spread, because I will keep pouring. You are beginning to notice. You are beginning to get wet. Be ready, be ready, be ready for My fresh outpouring. It's coming. It's coming. It's coming.

Day 38

Mercy & Truth

Let the trees of the forest rustle with praise before the Lord, for he is coming! He is coming to judge the earth. He will judge the world with justice, and the nations with his truth.
Psalm 96:12b-13 NLT

Yes, I know that judgment is a fearful word to you, not for yourself, for you are secure in My love, but you fear for others and for the earth. My justice will come, because I can't bear to see injustice in the earth forever.

Mercy and truth have met together; Righteousness and peace have kissed.
Psalm 85:10

Know that My truth does not come without mercy and My righteousness without peace. Do not fear, but be My witness. Don't shrink back, but push ahead. You are an agent of My mercy and peace. You are part of the healing river of My love. Flow with Me wherever I take you.

Waiting

Waiting is such a hard concept for you. Be at peace. When you wait on Me it's not a waste of time. You cannot be productive outside of My will. The wait is sometimes necessary. See it like a mill dam. Sometimes the water has to be dammed up in order to build up greater power. You will know the season when it's time to open the dam. I will show you. Be guided in everything by My Spirit.

Wait for the LORD;
be strong and take heart
and wait for the LORD.
Psalm 27:14 NIV

Day 40

Ears to hear

Tell Me if you have ears to hear. Do you hear only My rebuke? Do you hear only My praise? I want you to have ears to hear both. Do not shrink from the whole counsel of God. My rebuke is like oil for your head, and My praise is the grace I give to the humble. Both are for your good. I am your shepherd and I lead you in paths of righteousness. You must hear both My yes and My no. Hear My "yes, go this way" and My "no, don't go that way." If you can't hear both, you will go astray. My rebuke and praise are simply to train you and lead you, not to crush you or manipulate you. See, I am the good shepherd who lays down his life for his sheep.

Earthquakes

About midnight Paul and Silas were praying and singing hymns to God, and the prisoners were listening to them, and suddenly there was a great earthquake, so that the foundations of the prison were shaken, and immediately all the doors were opened, and everyone's bonds were unfastened.
Acts 16:25-26 ESV

The earth is mine. I use everything for My purposes. Do you fear natural disasters? Do you fear the loss of control? If you abide in Me, you need not fear anything. I saw Paul and Silas wounded and in prison. When they raised their hearts above the circumstances and began to pray and sing, I was so pleased with them that I shook the earth to free them.

Day 42

Without limit

He whom God has sent utters the words of God, for he gives the Spirit without limit.
John 3:34 ESV

I want to stretch you. Prepare to receive My Spirit without limit. What can you do to prepare? Prepare by opening your heart wide to receive from Me. You see, your spirit within you is like a new balloon. It is tight and needs to be loosened up. You also have many things that block My Spirit from flowing through your life: fears and protective walls, the need to be in control, anger and frustration. Are you willing to have Me work in your life? Do you want to have a fuller measure of My Spirit flowing through you? I am willing to give you the Spirit without limit. Be willing to have Me stretch you and open up your spirit. Trust Me. Cast every care on Me for I care for you. Receive from Me right now.

Limits

Limits of resources, limits of perseverance, limits of patience, peace and joy; these do not exist in heaven. Earthly existence is bound by limits, but you are not of this world. You are seated above in heavenly places. See the abundance of your home in heaven. *I have come that you may have life and have it more abundantly (John 10:10)*. I open the windows of heaven. You are the carrier of My abundance. Open up your heart to let the heavenly abundance flow down to earth. I pour it out, but will you see it and catch it? Do you lack anything that I desire for you? Come and receive it. Your heart is the connecting point between heaven and earth. You are the channel through which My abundance comes. Open wide in faith. Direct My flow to the area of lack.

Bring the full tithes into the storehouse, that there may be food in My house. And thereby put me to the test, says the LORD of hosts, if I will not open the windows of heaven for you and pour down for you a blessing until there is no more need.
Malachi 3:10 ESV

Day 44

Glory & Power

Yes I showed you two lessons from the weather, one about glory the other about power. When My glory falls on something that is not dead, it is destructive. Even as a blanket of snow fell on leaves that had not yet died off, bringing down whole trees, so My glory does not do well on human attitudes that are not dead to the flesh. Shed all pride, self-seeking and desire for the praise of man and allow Me to bring winter seasons into your life so that you may be ready for My glory. I also wanted you to see that My power is made perfect in weakness. A snow flake, what could be weaker. It melts when it lands on your nose. Yet, many of these weak bodies in unity can accomplish much. So is My Church. Each one of you is a small part, but when you are all in one accord and in one place, your unity becomes a weapon and you can demolish strongholds.

Courage

Christ died for us so that, whether we are dead or alive when he returns, we can live with him forever. So encourage each other and build each other up, just as you are already doing.
1 Thessalonians 5:10, 11 NLT

I have done My part, now you can do your part: to encourage each other and build each other up. You will experience heaven on earth when you do this. My people will be a light in the darkness. This sets you apart from the world. When you take the time to build yourself up in your most holy faith, you will have what it takes to build up others. How do you build yourself up? By praying in the Spirit. This is a small thing you do daily which results in a big change over time. You become a source of courage for others and a participant in the Kingdom of God.

Day 46

Looking

... looking unto Jesus, the author and finisher of our faith... Hebrews 12:2a

When you look unto Me, when you focus on Me and open your heart to Me, I will take care of everything that concerns faith. You can say to Me, "Lord, I believe, help my unbelief." It is not a contradiction, for you believe in Me, yet you see your own weak faith. That is enough. That is the mustard seed-sized faith you need. Look to Me. Believe that I am and that I am a rewarder of those who diligently seek Me. That is enough. I will take care of designing your faith, of building it, of polishing it, of bringing it to completion. I will stretch it when it needs to be stretched, but your faith is never separate of Me. Don't trust in your faith, trust in Me. Come close to Me and walk with Me, and you will be confident that you are going in the right direction.

Funnel

*And now the word of the Lord is ringing out from
you to people everywhere...*
1 Thessalonians 1:8a NLT

My word is ringing out and gathering in. As I have
built My Church in the past, so I build My Church
now. My Church is like a funnel, funneling people to
Me. I am causing people to be drawn in. This is a
new day and I am doing a new work. Be ready for
many, not one or two, here or there, but many
souls seeking My presence, My salvation and My
love. It is like the multiplication of the loaves and
fishes. My disciples were willing to begin the process
of passing out the little they had, and I did the
miracle of multiplication. If you are willing to do
whatever you can, I will add My power to your small
effort and it will multiply. And as they begin to
come, others will be swept in with them. The
current of inflow will be supernatural and sovereign.

*Enlarge the place of your tent, and let them stretch
out the curtains of your dwellings; Do not spare;
Lengthen your cords, and strengthen your stakes.
Isaiah 54:2*

Day 48

Overflow

You anoint my head with oil; my cup overflows.
Psalm 23:5b

I am the God of more than enough. Make room in
your life for My overflow. You can have more than
enough love, more than enough patience, more
than enough grace for every situation in your life
and for every person you relate to. Look at My life.
Did I ever run out of love? No, I loved to the death.
I gave and continued to give. So your life can be.
What hinders you from My abundance? Can you not
receive it, or have you not learned how to pour it
out? Seek after both. Receive and give. The reason I
say that it is better to give than to receive is
because in giving you make more room to receive.
So today, receive from Me the anointing you need
and then give out love, give out patience, give out
healing, give out blessing, give out wisdom, give out
encouragement and strength. You can do what I
did: go around doing good and healing all who are
oppressed by the devil. I am with you.

And you know that God anointed Jesus of Nazareth
with the Holy Spirit and with power. Then Jesus
went around doing good and healing all who were
oppressed by the devil, for God was with him.
Acts 10:38 NLT

Understand & Know

Thus says the LORD: "Let not the wise man boast in his wisdom, let not the mighty man boast in his might, let not the rich man boast in his riches, but let him who boasts boast in this, that he understands and knows me, that I am the LORD who practices steadfast love, justice, and righteousness in the earth. For in these things I delight, declares the LORD."
Jeremiah 9:23-24 ESV

Oh that My people would understand and know Me. You know Me only as much as you focus in on Me. I am not aloof and I don't hold back My heart from you. When you focus in, past all distractions, you will know more and more of My steadfast, unfailing love. When you press into Me you will learn how mercy and truth, righteousness and peace work together in Me. These are times of testing for many, times of sifting. Press into Me, abide in Me and abide in My unfailing love. Let your selfish attitudes, your ambitions and all other distractions be sifted away and simply come to Me and delight with Me in love, justice and righteousness.

Day 50

Rest

Rest, yes, take a moment to rest in Me. Come into the shelter of My everlasting peace. Let the oil of My presence soothe your nerves and cover you from the harshness of the world. You are in this world, but you are not of it. You have resources unknown to this world. You have Me. My Spirit lives within you and gives you peace, strength, love and joy. Draw from Me all that you need. You must see yourself as separate from the world, being supplied by Me. You are like a smuggler. You are bringing secret weapons into this world from heaven. Your secret weapons are peace, strength, love and joy.

Unprecedented

I will pour out My Spirit in an unprecedented way.
You will go about business as usual, when suddenly
everything will change. You will know it and you will
see it. When a flash flood suddenly comes, you can't
deny it or hide it. Do not be concerned with your
plans. Just stay close to Me, listen for My voice, stay
strong in your faith, and don't let yourself be
pushed off course now. Persevere in doing good.
Continue to desire My presence in your life and in
the Church. As you listen to the Spirit within you
and speak those things which are not, you are
drawing Me in to act.

Day 52

Prayer

The word prayer is like the word conversation. A conversation can have many different forms and topics, and so the word prayer describes many different activities. It is a conversation between you and Me. You wonder if your prayer is pleasing to Me. Just think about when a conversation is pleasing to you. It's when you connect on a heart level, when you talk and listen and communicate, when you understand and are understood. It's the same with prayer. I am pleased when you connect with My heart. When you listen to Me, and when you come to Me for better understanding of My ways and My wisdom. I like it when you're honest with Me about your concerns and feelings. I also like it when you speak those things into existence that I show you. When your faith connects with My will, you will speak those things which are not as though they were and they will be. So come, listen first and then speak.

Why?

You ask, "Why do you love me?" I love you because you are My child. I have a deep interest in everything that concerns you. I am ever watching for anything you think or do that will bring Me joy. I watch for

...whatever things are true, whatever things are noble, whatever things are just, whatever things are pure, whatever things are lovely, whatever things are of good report, if there is any virtue and if there is anything praiseworthy.
Philippians 4:8

When I see these things in you I am pleased.

I also loved you when your back was turned to Me. Then I prayed that the heart of the child would be turned to the Father. My longing will draw you ever back to Me.

I also love you when you struggle. At those times My heart hurts with you, not because I have no hope, but because I long for My hope to be in you.

The best for Me is when you love Me with all your heart, soul and strength, when your heart is tender towards Me and you receive all that I have for you.

Day 54

Diamond

For whoever wants to save his life will lose it, but whoever loses his life for Me and for the gospel will save it.
Mark 8:35 NIV

You know this principle, I have taught it to you from the beginning. Whatever you hang onto and hoard, you will lose, but whatever you release and give freely, you will gain. It's the same with your will. If you stubbornly insist on your own will, it will become hard and brittle.

I will bless those who have humble and contrite hearts, who tremble at My word. But those who choose their own ways, delighting in their sins, are cursed... I will send great troubles against them--all the things they feared. For when I called, they did not answer. When I spoke, they did not listen. They deliberately sinned--before My very eyes--and chose to do what they know I despise.
Isaiah 66:2b-4 NLT

I had mercy on you, and you have learned to yield your will to Me. You have said, *"not my will but your will be done."* Though your heart is contrite and soft towards Me, in that very place of your soul I am making you hard as a diamond to resist evil. Be soft towards Me, lose your life towards Me and you will gain My will, My zeal and My strength.

I am here!

I was ready to be sought by those who did not ask for me; I was ready to be found by those who did not seek me. I said, "Here am I, here am I," to a nation that was not called by my name.
Isaiah 65:1 ESV

Yes, I am here! I have made a way for those who want Me. I long for My lost sheep. All people belong to Me, and I long for all to know Me. The time is now! I will be found by many who were not even looking for Me, because My heart longs for them and My heart draws them. Why do I long for them so? Because I love them and unless they come to Me, they will not know that love. They are harassed like sheep without a shepherd. They neither know My love nor My protection. They are walking blindly into trouble. They do not know the way of salvation. They do not know the disaster awaiting those who are not protected by eternal life. Those who hear Me, come! Here is what I long for, that you would open your heart and receive My free gift of salvation, receive eternal life. You say that you don't understand? Understand My love for you! You don't see all that I see. I see the past, the present and the future. I see what is needed for your protection. Have you always done what is best for you? No, because you have not always known the way. I do know the way. I am the way. If you trust in Me, you can never go wrong.

Day 56

Burdens

Yes, I see the things that press in on you, but I see them differently than you do. You see stresses, concerns for others, unrighteousness and injustice as burdens that you find hard to carry. I see them as training weights. I will not give you more than you can carry and I see how you are getting stronger because I have allowed these things in your life. Nothing can come that I haven't allowed, so seek My wisdom in how to deal with each difficulty. In everything I will supply you with wisdom, with strength, even with joy. Your joy does not come from dropping your burden, but from lifting it up to Me and overcoming your problem in faith. Everything is designed to stretch your faith in Me. As you trust Me, you overcome and you gain more of My life in you. Receive My joy now. My joy is your strength. It gives you the ability to stand up under the weight of your burdens. Receive My joy like new wine into your soul.

Pressed

When fatigue, stress and hurry seem to crush the very life out of you, come to Me. You say you can't? You are overwhelmed and pressed down? I know what it's like to be pressed down by the cross you carry. I was overwhelmed and I was unable to bear the cross by myself. Simon of Cyrene helped Me.

Are you ashamed when you are weak? Despise the shame and accept the help I will send you. It is My law, which I have written on your heart, that you bear one another's burden. I have made you to need one another. Then together you can come to Me and I will give you rest and strength.

Bear one another's burdens, and so fulfill the law of Christ.
Galatians 6:2 ESV

Day 58

Fresh Start

Come to me with your ears wide open. Listen, for the life of your soul is at stake... Seek the Lord while you can find him. Call on him now while he is near. Let the people turn from their wicked deeds. Let them banish from their minds the very thought of doing wrong! Let them turn to the Lord that he may have mercy on them. Yes, turn to our God, for he will abundantly pardon.
Isaiah 55:3a,6 NLT

If only My people knew how eager I am to give them a fresh start. I can completely cut them off from their past: "Neither will I condemn you - Go and sin no more," and all is forgiven, all is new, and they can press on to the high calling. My heart is for your future. Forget about the past. Regret is not a path you can walk on. It's full of snares and sharp rocks. Walk on the path I show you, it is paved with faith, hope and love. It is the path of grace and obedience.

Valley

Live a life filled with love for others, following the example of Christ, who loved you and gave himself as a sacrifice to take away your sins. And God was pleased, because that sacrifice was like sweet perfume to him.
Ephesians 5:2 NLT

And so your sacrifice of love will please God. How do you offer up a sacrifice of love? By repaying evil with good; By countering pride with humility; By going low in order to reach the high calling of God. I lead you through the valley. You can't get to the next mountain without going through this valley, so be thankful for the valley, because without it you could not reach the next stop on your journey. This is where I will show myself strong. This is where you become like Me. Now is the time to die to your own ideas about what is good for you and embrace Me. I am good for you. *I am the way, the truth and the life.* Shake yourself loose from any ideology that is not of Me. Get yourself ready. I'm excited because now we get to run.

Lay aside every weight, and the sin which so easily ensnares us, and let us run with endurance the race that is set before us.
*Hebrews 12:1*b

Day 60

Despised

*For we are to God the aroma of Christ among those
who are being saved and those who are perishing.
To the one we are the smell of death; to the other,
the fragrance of life.*
2 Corinthians 2:15 NIV

Beauty is in the eye of the beholder. Don't be
concerned with how others perceive you. Just be My
fragrance of love, of wisdom, of grace and of peace.
If your peace is received by another, be available. If
your peace is rejected, move on. Do not fear
rejection for it is part of being My servant. It's hard
for a sensitive soul to endure rejection and insults,
but I have given you My life. Part of My life is to
despise the shame of rejection. What do I mean by
that? I despised the shame, I endured it and I
counted it worth the prize. I didn't let concern over
being shamed and rejected stop Me from finishing
what the Father called Me to. I died to the need of
being accepted by those who were perishing. I
despised the shame, knowing that if I endured, I
would gain the prize. And you are that prize.

*...looking unto Jesus, the author and finisher of our
faith, who for the joy that was set before Him
endured the cross, despising the shame, and has
sat down at the right hand of the throne of God.*
Hebrews 12:2

Supply

My supply of grace and peace for you is greater than you will ever need. You can never have a circumstance in your life that exceeds the capacity of My grace and peace. My supply in comparison to your need is like Lake Erie compared with your need for water. You cannot possibly use it all or run out, but you do need to come to Me and receive. When you are anxious it simply means you are thirsty for My grace and peace.

"If anyone thirsts, let him come to Me and drink. Whoever believes in Me, as the Scripture has said, 'Out of his heart will flow rivers of living water.'"
Now this he said about the Spirit, whom those who believed in him were to receive...
John 7:37b-39a

I am your maker and I love you. I will allow circumstances to press you so that you recognize your need for My grace, My peace, My love and My power. Your need is there before trials happen in your life, but it is covered up by distractions. When you are pressed, your need rises to the surface. Your soul begins to cry out, and when you cry out to Me and come to Me, the supply I give you is not just enough for yourself, but it will flow out from you like a river to quench the thirst of others.

Day 62

Fullness

And I pray that Christ will be more and more at home in your hearts as you trust in him. May your roots go down deep into the soil of God's marvelous love. And may you have the power to understand, as all God's people should, how wide, how long, how high, and how deep his love really is. May you experience the love of Christ, though it is so great you will never fully understand it. Then you will be filled with the fullness of life and power that comes from God.
Ephesians 3:17-19 NLT

Fullness of life, that's what I want for you. Fullness of life and power come when I am fully at home in your heart. When you allow Me into every part of your heart and when My life within you, My love within you and My power within you grows of its own. When a seed falls into the soil, the life within that seed begins to expand. First it cracks the old protective outer shell which is no longer needed. Then it sprouts up with new life and power. The roots grow down, the new life grows up. Continual nourishment produces continual growth, vigor and power. The nourishment I provide for you is My love. My love is big. Your roots will never grow too large for the container of My love. Even as you don't know the limits of the universe, so you don't know the limits of My love. You may not understand it, but you can experience it. Let the life of My love take hold of you.

Favor

May God be merciful and bless us. May his face shine with favor upon us.
Psalm 67:1b

Yes, My favor shines on all who look to Me in faith. When faith, as small as a seed, begins to grow in the heart, I am so eager and so excited to watch. I am like a woman who discovers she is pregnant. I know the seed is small, but I see so much more. I have expectations of a whole life lived in faith. Once the seed is in the heart, it's a done deal. It will grow. It will mature, and I will do all to protect and to nurture that seed. Therefore, if anyone is in Christ, he is a new creation. The old has passed away; behold, the new has come. Yes, the new has come.

He died for everyone so that those who receive his new life will no longer live to please themselves. Instead, they will live to please Christ, who died and was raised for them.
2 Corinthians 5:15 NLT

Day 64

Grace and Peace

May grace and peace be multiplied to you in the knowledge of God and of Jesus our Lord.
2 Peter 1:2 ESV

Grace and peace are always available to you. They are always on their way to you, like a radio station that plays only grace and peace. Are you tuned in? My signal is constant and unfailing. *My grace is sufficient for you*. It can't be interrupted by anything. No lack of grace in you can ever be attributed to Me, for I am always transmitting it to you. If there is any lack of grace or peace or power, it's because you've tuned out. You've become distracted, stopped receiving and you've stopped relying on My Spirit within you. Just tune back in. The quicker you learn to recognize a weak signal, the quicker you return to full power. I love you and I am giving you *everything you need for life and godliness*. Everything! *Nothing can separate you from My love*, at least nothing external. You are the only one who can tune Me out.

Anchor

This hope is a strong and trustworthy anchor for our souls. It leads us through the curtain into God's inner sanctuary. Jesus has already gone in there for us. He has become our eternal High Priest in the order of Melchizedek.
Hebrews 6:19-20 NLT

Follow Me. Follow Me into the Father's inner sanctuary. All is open and available to those who follow Me, *for I am the way and the truth and the life. No one comes to the Father except through Me.* I have put eternity in your heart, and that eternity longs for and belongs, not to this world, but to the Kingdom of God. There are no rules or rituals you must follow in order to find the way. Simply come. *Draw near to God and he will draw near to you.* Come near to Me and I will show you the way.

Day 66

Circumstances

Circumstances, those external, earthly things that surround you, try to create in you feelings that gnaw at your soul. Fear, anxiety, frustration, anger, hopelessness, and confusion, these are all emotions that are destructive to you. They come so natural, but you are not subject to your old nature.

For you have been called to live in freedom, my brothers and sisters. But don't use your freedom to satisfy your sinful nature. Instead, use your freedom to serve one another in love.
Galatians 5:13 NLT

Let not your external circumstances control your soul, but let My internal Spirit exude his influence. Let My Spirit within you expand and take control where you feel that you have lost control. I allow the circumstances so that you learn to rely on Me and draw from Me the power and strength of soul to overcome the world. Great miracles happen in your soul when you consistently resist destructive forces in the power of My Spirit.

I have said these things to you, that in Me you may have peace. In the world you will have tribulation. But take heart; I have overcome the world.
John 16:33 ESV

Justice

Yes, I see all that is evil. I see every hurt that is inflicted. I see every deception, and I see all injustice. All that is evil grieves Me and makes Me angry. I curb My anger every day, for the time is not yet. I am not a disinterested bystander of the affairs of this world. I gave everything so that whosoever believes in Me should not perish but have eternal life. I gave everything I had in heaven, and I gave everything I had on earth. I laid down My glorious might, and I laid down My life. Yet they perish. Yet they go on without Me. There is still time for salvation and a little more time for grace.

Behold My servant, whom I uphold, My chosen, in whom My soul delights; I have put My Spirit upon him; he will bring forth justice to the nations. He will not cry aloud or lift up his voice, or make it heard in the street; a bruised reed he will not break, and a faintly burning wick he will not quench; he will faithfully bring forth justice. He will not grow faint or be discouraged till he has established justice in the earth; and the coastlands wait for his law. Thus says God, the LORD, …: "I am the LORD; I have called you in righteousness; I will take you by the hand and keep you; I will give you as a covenant for the people, a light for the nations, to open the eyes that are blind, to bring out the prisoners from the dungeon, from the prison those who sit in darkness.
Isaiah 42:1-7 ESV

Day 68

Time

How precious to Me is the time you offer Me. Time to commune and be together. Time when My Spirit within you is free to breathe out to you all that is of Me. All of Me is available to you. This is why I endured the cross so that I could pour My love on you and know that it is received. My love pours out regardless, but My joy comes from knowing it's received. I jealously guard this intimate time. I move heaven and earth to have it, not only because it brings Me joy, but because it is your life flow. This abiding is what makes you alive and strong, vigorous and resilient, gracious and loving. In this abiding you find wisdom and understanding, counsel and might, knowledge and the fear of the LORD. Here you receive love, joy, peace, patience, kindness, goodness, faithfulness, gentleness and self-control. Are you low on patience? Then come and receive more. Are you low on peace? It's available to you. All I have for all you need.

I also receive from you. I receive your love and your gratitude. I receive your faith as a gift when you trust in Me. I receive your hope and your thanksgiving. I gladly receive your praise and your worship because then you open your heart for more of Me. Through the overflow of this abiding, your service to Me and to your brothers and sisters becomes a gift as well.

Repentance

When you have a sense of failure or disappointment in yourself, think soberly. The work of repentance is not just to forget what happened, but to see clearly where you have gone wrong. Mark the way that leads to destruction so you recognize it when temptation leads you there again. Plan ahead so next time you will detour the dangerous road. See each temptation as a slippery slope. Set your mark on the very first step you took over the edge, on the very first thought of desire. Mark where you turned away from Me and walked on your own. And above all, do not get bogged down in condemnation. I want you to keep moving forward. My grace will pull you out of the ditch. Let not your pride keep you wallowing. Trust Me and see My hand pulling you up and out. I forgive you, I cleanse you, and I set you back on the right road. Stay in My presence and walk with Me.

Day 70

Strength

My power is made perfect in your weakness. How does that happen? It happens when, in your weakness, you look to Me. It happens when you say to yourself, *"Why so downcast oh my soul, put your hope in God."* Never for one moment is My strength not available to you. My strength is in who I am. If you come near to Me, you'll have My strength. You'll have My strength to overcome temptation. You'll have My strength to persevere with grace in situations that disturb you. You'll have My strength to set your mind on things above not on things of the earth. I will give you My strength.

In the world you will have tribulation. But take heart; I have overcome the world.
John 16:33b ESV

Shine

I am with you. I am near you. You are a window of heaven. You are a carrier of My presence. Each one who has received My light is a window through which that light shines into a dark world. Keep your window open, and keep My light burning inside.

Arise, shine, for your light has come, and the glory of the LORD has risen upon you. For behold, darkness shall cover the earth, and thick darkness the peoples; but the LORD will arise upon you, and his glory will be seen upon you. And nations shall come to your light, and kings to the brightness of your rising.
Isaiah 60:1-3 ESV

Many will come and many will see the light that is shining from My people. Let nothing interfere with your light. Be quick to remove all that is not of Me from your heart, all self-seeking, anger and frustration. Cast your cares on Me because I care for you and I know how they interfere with the light that is in you. Now is the time to shine.

Day 72

Praises

O my Strength, to you I sing praises, for you, O God, are my refuge, the God who shows me unfailing love.
Psalm 59:17 NLT

Yes, as you sing praises, you open the gates into the tower of My refuge where you will find My unfailing love. Your spirit needs the strength of My refuge in order to be vulnerable enough to receive My love. This is My goal for you, that you would know My unfailing love; that you would seek it, know it, receive it, possess it, live it, and pour it out. Unfailing, what does that mean to you? It never falls short. It never becomes selfish. It always pours out. It doesn't look for something in return. Unfailing, it never stops. Your own love and strength will fall short, but My unfailing love is ever flowing, ever working, ever saving, and ever expanding. It conquers all.

I will bless the LORD at all times; his praise shall continually be in my mouth.
Psalm 34:1b ESV

Satisfied

My soul shall be satisfied as with marrow and fatness,
And my mouth shall praise You with joyful lips.
Psalm 63:5

I came that they may have life and have it abundantly.
John 10:10b ESV

That life is what satisfies your soul. My life force flowing into you nurtures you and changes you. When you come to Me and are filled up with Me, you'll have everything you need in abundance. You'll have more than enough love, more than enough grace, more than enough peace and more than enough joy. You'll have enough to share with those around you. You won't have to be stingy. I am here for you NOW. My Spirit longs to supply you. It is My nature to pour out, and as you are supplied by Me, it will be your nature to pour out. Just as water flows to the lowest point, My Spirit flows to the point of need.

Needy Soul

You have wondered, "Why have you made me to be so needy in my soul?" You are needy because I desire to show forth My power through you. As the Dead Sea is needy for water because it is the lowest point on the earth, so your soul is needy. Do not be confused by that. When you receive only what is earthly, your soul turns bitter, just as the Dead Sea. But you have tapped into Me.

He said to me, "This water flows toward the eastern region and goes down into the Arabah (the Jordan Valley), where it enters the Sea (the Dead Sea). When it empties into the Sea (the Dead Sea), the water there becomes fresh. Swarms of living creatures will live wherever the river flows. There will be large numbers of fish, because this water flows there and makes the salt water fresh; so where the river flows everything will live. Fishermen will stand along the shore; from En Gedi to En Eglaim there will be places for spreading nets. The fish will be of many kinds—like the fish of the Great Sea (the Mediterranean). But the swamps and marshes will not become fresh; they will be left for salt. Fruit trees of all kinds will grow on both banks of the river. Their leaves will not wither, nor will their fruit fail. Every month they will bear, because the water from the sanctuary flows to them. Their fruit will serve for food and their leaves for healing."
Ezekiel 47:8-12 NIV

Harvesters

Unless the LORD builds the house, they labor in vain who build it; Unless the LORD guards the city, the watchman stays awake in vain.
Psalm 127:1

Your protection goes beyond what human watchmen can do. As long as there are those who acknowledge their weaknesses and cry out to Me for help, I will guard your city and your country. I give grace to the humble, but I oppose the proud. Even as Abraham came to know, if there are ten who are righteous, for their sake I will spare the city. If there is a remnant that calls on Me and seeks My face, I will help. Cry out to Me for help, keep on asking and keep on knocking. I see the harvesters gathering, and for their sake I will guard this place.

First of all, then, I urge that supplications, prayers, intercessions, and thanksgivings be made for all people, for kings and all who are in high positions, that we may lead a peaceful and quiet life, godly and dignified in every way. This is good, and it is pleasing in the sight of God our Savior, who desires all people to be saved and to come to the knowledge of the truth.
1 Timothy 2:1-2 ESV

Day 76

Unity

Don't let yourself be moved from the path I have for you, either by praise or by criticism. I direct your steps. I have a plan and I have a future for you. If you receive affirmation or correction, receive it only as long as it brings you forward on My path for you. Don't let it turn you back or sidetrack you. Keep going forward. Yes, even praise can hinder you if it causes you to become too conscious of the opinions of the one who praised you. Do everything as unto Me. Look to My affirmation first. Let My will, let My direction and affirmation flow so mightily in your life that all other opinions by comparison are just a little trickle.

He yearns jealously over the spirit that He has made to dwell in us.
James 4:5b ESV

I yearn jealously over your heart, your attention and your affections. I have bought you by My blood. Others do not have the same claim on you. You are actually mine. And I know that you long for My direction and My presence, so keep your heart and soul free from entanglements. Flow together with others who are free like you and who follow My will. You will accomplish much as you flow together in unity. That unity and oneness can only happen between people who put Me first. It is by My Spirit.

Unlimited

I am with you always, but you are not with Me always. Whenever you open your spirit, My manifested presence comes. Whenever your spirit is not open and eager for Me, I do not show myself. In My presence is fullness of joy, so as soon as you are open and abide, there is joy. Learn to abide, not only when all is quiet, but in the middle of your busyness. I have trained you to have a quiet time with Me so you would learn how to enter My presence. Now I want to train you to enter My presence at other times. All through the day, My joy is available to you. All through the day you can receive from Me and give to others. When you abide in Me, you have an unlimited supply of everything that is good.

For the one whom God has sent speaks the words of God, for God gives the Spirit without limit. The Father loves the Son and has placed everything in his hands.
John 3:34-35 NIV

Day 78

Abundance

With every breath you can exchange the divine for the human. With every breath you can take in Me and breathe out you. I will increase and you will decrease. The Spirit will come and the flesh will go. Receive Me; breathe Me, every day, every hour, every minute, and every second. The great exchange happens continually: more of Me, less of you.

Breathe in love, breathe out rejection.
Breathe in faith, breathe out fear.
Breathe in hope, breathe out despair.
Breathe in grace, breathe out condemnation.
Breathe in truth, breathe out confusion.

My gifts for you are without limit. All you need to do is consciously receive them. My gifts and My love are like Niagara Falls. They flow in absolute abundance at all times. Yet your life often is so distracted or focused on the need that you're not open to the flow. You're like a bottle with a small opening held under the falls. Sometimes you're not even right-side-up. Look to Me, open wide and receive Me abundantly.

Changes

Let it go. Let it go. You can no more make yourself
to be fearless than to be selfless. Just keep crying
out to Me. I am the one who changes you from
glory to glory by My Spirit. Bring every shortcoming
to Me and be glad that you need Me. Be glad of
every little thing that reminds you to come to Me.
For I yearn to be with you. I long for constant
communion with your heart. That's why My power is
made perfect in your weakness. I perfect you each
time you come to Me. You may not even know what
I do for you. You may come for one reason and I
see another area I want to help you with. So just
stay near and be happy. Just come close and let Me
feed you with My joy.

*And I am sure of this, that he who began a good
work in you will bring it to completion at the day of
Jesus Christ.*
Philippians 1:6 ESV

Compassion

Fear not. Why would I say that if I didn't know that you have the natural tendency to fear? I say, fear not. Being able to step beyond fear in obedience to My Word, that is the great test of faith. Step through the barrier. You have won smaller tests of faith by being on the defense, but the great test of faith comes only when you go on the offense. When you take the steps to go out and do the things you know I want you to do. Defensive living, keeping yourself from doing wrong, is only a small part of My plan for you.

You see yourself as having little strength to go on the offense. What about, "When I am weak then I am strong." Are you willing to trust Me? Are you willing to invest your one talent, offer it up to Me, and let Me use it and multiply it? Did you not once feel weak in other areas, and have I not multiplied whatever gift you have given Me? So give Me what you have. Give Me your empathy for others, and I will turn it into true compassion, compassion that does something about their state. I will flow through your empathy into those you touch. Take your eyes off of what you don't have and where you feel weak, and focus on Me and My desire to use what you have. Simply be available for Me to flow through. The tools I give you are like a garden hose. Simply be willing to go to the dry places, hold it, point it and let Me flow through it.

Eternal Life

He who has the Son has life.
1 John 5:12 NIV

When you have Me, you have life. I don't even look at life without Me as real life, because without Me the spirit of man is not yet alive. When you have Me, my life pulses in you. Eternity has been awakened in you. You can either nurture that life or you can let it be deprived and malnourished.

...they who wait for the LORD shall renew their strength;
Isaiah 40:31

Your soul is hungry and thirsty for the life you receive from waiting on Me. When you open your soul and drink in My presence, it nurtures the life that is within you. My life – which is to say – My grace is sufficient for every need you have. Your needs activate My life and grace in you, if you wait on Me. Understand this, it's important: Every need and deprivation you feel in your soul can be a conduit for more of Me. If you let every little thing that bothers you turn you to Me, your needs will be met in the most amazing ways. Not maybe in the way you think, because My ways are higher than your ways and My thoughts higher than yours. Your needs and wants, if focused on Me, create the necessary force to bring more of My life into you.

Day 82

Hunger & Thirst

If a baby would not feel hunger, it would not want its mother and it would not grow. Does the baby know all that happens to its body and soul because of what it does while nursing? No. Does the baby like the feeling of hunger that causes it to cry out for its mother? No. Your dissatisfaction, your hunger and your thirst are an intricate part of the life I have given you. I want you to feel them, because without them you would not turn to Me and gain from Me that with which I designed and desire to nurture you. My life flows from My presence.

Blessed are those who hunger and thirst for righteousness for they shall be satisfied.
Matthew 5:6 *NIV*

And I mean satisfied each time you let Me nurture you with My righteousness. It's not a onetime thing. You will hunger and thirst for righteousness until the Son of Righteousness returns. It is one of the ways that I do a good work in you now. It will be completed on the day I return.

"If anyone thirsts, let him come to Me and drink. Whoever believes in Me, as the Scripture has said, 'Out of his heart will flow rivers of living water.'"
John 7:37b-38 ESV

Plans

I walk the path of your destiny; stay close to Me and walk with Me.

You don't have to worry about the future or about making many plans, because I have plans for you. I have a future and a hope for you. All you need to aim for is to walk with Me. All you need to be concerned about is to stay close to Me. Isn't that much easier than to try and figure out all possible outcomes ahead of time and to plan for all contingencies?

Now is the time of importance. Now is when I want you to listen for My voice and let Me guide you. If you trust Me with each little step, I take care that you follow the big plans I have for you.

Day 84

Oneness

You are coming into a greater oneness with Me. As you grow in fullness, as I mature your spirit and as you allow My Spirit to transform your mind, your will and your emotion, you are coming into greater oneness with Me. You are becoming solid—solid in faith. When My people go through death to themselves, they become at first very vulnerable, but I continue to do My work and as each part of the old dies, it is replaced by the life and strength of the new. Not only are you in greater oneness with Me, but as you allow My Spirit to rule your spirit, your soul and your body, you are in greater oneness within yourself. Tough you may experience the rising up of the flesh, it happens less and less the more you give full authority to the Spirit. Your quick obedience brings peace and joy. And not only are you in greater oneness with Me, but you will be in greater oneness with My other children. Only those who have died to themselves can be a part of the oneness in the Spirit. The oneness connection starts in the heart. From there it grows and matures. I delight in the oneness of My children. That's why I come whenever two or more are gathered in My name. When you are with others and your spirits open up in prayer or worship, then I am drawn to you like a magnet.

Immeasurable

*That is why we never give up. Though our bodies
are dying; our spirits are being renewed every day.
For our present troubles are quite small and won't
last very long. Yet they produce for us an
immeasurably great glory that will last forever.*
2 Corinthians 4:16-17 NLT

I am working on your inside. Let everything that
happens to you, every frustration, confusion or
deprivation bring you closer to Me. Let everything
cause you to be more open to My help, My joy, My
supply, My hope and My love. As you cast down
your cares and let Me fill you with hope and faith, I
build you up for eternity. I form you now for eternal
glory. You will see why Paul said, "Count it all joy."
For the very things you would avoid in the natural
will cause you to grow in the spirit. Every battle
makes you stronger if you are focused on Me. Every
challenge gives you more creativity if you are open
to My wisdom. Every situation becomes an
opportunity for a miracle if you trust in Me. As you
abide in Me, you are being renewed deep inside. I
am changing you NOW into a being with
immeasurable glory. And that glory will last forever.
It's not yet visible, but it will be one day.

Day 86

Directions

The LORD preserves those with knowledge, but he ruins the plans of the treacherous.
Proverbs 22:12 NLT

I direct all. I direct the godly and the ungodly. I preserve and guide and build up the godly, but I oppose and humble the ungodly, and I ruin their plans. I do all in you by the guiding of My Spirit. Step by step My Spirit guides you, not only in big leaps, but in every little step. Follow My guiding even if you have never before set step in the direction I send you. I have walked before you and know the way. Trust in Me and follow Me. Do not fear, simply follow. I will show you the pitfalls and the dangers. I will lead you around every obstacle. Trust in Me.

Reflection

And all of us have had that veil removed so that we can be mirrors that brightly reflect the glory of the Lord. And as the Spirit of the Lord works within us, we become more and more like him and reflect his glory even more.
2 Corinthians 3:18 NLT

You are My people, and you reflect Me. You reflect My glory, My goodness and My power. You reflect Me into the dark places where I have not yet been invited. Your very beings bring Me into view of those who are My sheep, but don't know Me yet. They have not seen Me, but you make My glory visible to them. You bring light and love and joy. You bring truth and righteousness into view. You make love and mercy visible. There are those who want to crack your mirrors, but I have protected you. My Spirit causes you to be in unity within My sheepfold. Guard that unity. In a telescope, many mirrors, polished and adjusted just right, bring far off objects into perfect view. So it is that I will use My Church to bring Me into perfect view.

Day 88

Protection

Don't let your heart be troubled. I will show you what to do when you become confused or anxious. I will show you what to do when a false teaching tries to influence you like yeast. I am your good shepherd. I care for you. I guard you and I know how to cure you of any trouble or annoyance. Even as your physical body knows how to rid itself of things that don't agree with it, so your spirit needs to vomit up any falseness.

But I am afraid that just as Eve was deceived by the serpent's cunning, your minds may somehow be led astray from your sincere and pure devotion to Christ. For if someone comes to you and preaches a Jesus other than the Jesus we preached, or if you receive a different spirit from the one you received, or a different gospel from the one you accepted, you put up with it easily enough.
2 Corinthians 11:3-4 NIV

So I tell you, don't put up with anything that is not Me.

Shepherd

My sheep hear My voice, and I know them, and they follow Me.
John 10:27 ESV

You hear My voice. You know that I don't speak with condemnation. You know that I don't speak with accusation. Yes, the yeast of the Pharisees is still in the world, but I have given you everything you need to guard you. I have built My Church strong and with many watchtowers. I have given you true apostles, prophets, evangelists, pastors and teachers so that you will not be...

...tossed back and forth by the waves, and blown here and there by every wind of teaching and by the cunning and craftiness of men in their deceitful scheming.
Ephesians 4:14 NIV

Be glad in Me, be glad in My protection and be so very glad in the grace and freedom you have.

There is a river whose streams make glad the city of God, the holy habitation of the Most High. God is in the midst of her; she shall not be moved; God will help her when morning dawns.
Psalm 46:4-5 ESV

Day 90

Conflict

Resolve your conflicts without accusations. Do not jump to quick judgments and conclusions. Understand that your view of the situation is only partial. You cannot see the whole heart of another person. You cannot understand every motive. So when you evaluate a situation, at most you can give your opinion about it. Don't be deceived into thinking that your opinion is the whole truth. Step very lightly when you speak your concerns about a brother or sister. Never speak behind their backs, and when you speak to them directly, be very careful.

Who are you to pass judgment on the servant of another? It is before his own master that he stands or falls. And he will be upheld, for the Lord is able to make him stand.
Romans 14:4 ESV

If I am able to make him stand, don't be an instrument of the enemy to make him fall. Your words are powerful. Do not tear down your brother or sister, but help them to tear down strongholds. Build them up. Remove their stumbling blocks. Show them the right way. Lead them to the way of grace. I want you to understand the love I have for the person who annoys you. I see in them a potential for change. I am their potter and I use every situation, every trial, every difficulty to mold them into My image.

Affections

Set your affections on things above, not on things on the earth.
Colossians 3:2 KJV

I want you to do that. When you do, you leave behind limitations, weaknesses, difficulties and old hurts. I want you to think of each day as a brand new start without any baggage from the past.

Great is his faithfulness; his mercies begin afresh each morning.
Lamentation 3:23 NLT

As you look to the things that are above, I make them available to you. Set your affections, set your desires, set your wants and your needs on things above. Realize that what your heart wants and needs most of all is not what the earth has to offer in material things, in entertainment, in food, in busyness, even in affection from people. No, what your heart is most hungry and thirsty for can not to be found in the natural realm. Here is what will satisfy you: My presence; and with My presence everything I have stored up for your use. All that deeply satisfies your heart is with Me. When you draw near to Me, you draw near to what you need and want.

Day 92

Delight

Delight yourself in the LORD, and he will give you the desires of your heart.
Psalm 37:4 NIV

The desires of your heart are love, joy, peace, patience, kindness, goodness, faithfulness, gentleness and self-control. See this fruit of the Spirit not just as the necessary signs of maturity that help you get along with others. No, it is so much more.

This is fruit for your own good. Taste each one. Meditate on each one. This is heavenly food for you. It is My love that fills your heart with exquisite ecstasy.

It is My joy that bubbles up from you and makes you laugh and be strong and able to overcome the temporary troubles of life.

It is My peace that settles on you and keeps you calm. Think on each fruit and taste it today. As you do and become satisfied, it will benefit others as well.

Unfailing love

My love truly is unfailing. It was tested in the wilderness, it was tested in every interaction with people, and it was tested on the cross. I was willing to let it pour out of Me as blood. Are you willing to let it pour into and out of you?

Yes, I am the vine; you are the branches. Those who remain in Me, and I in them, will produce much fruit. For apart from Me you can do nothing.
John 15:5 NLT

You do not have unfailing love on your own. Your natural affection only works with people who love you back. Your nature is to be selfish and to think what you can get in return for your care. Unfailing love does not depend on any return. It flows only in one direction: from Me to you and from you to others. Let My love satisfy your heart and fill you to overflowing. It flows out like a river and will not return upstream. Yet there are others who will receive My unfailing love and let it overflow to you. So be open to the best things. Be open to the love that comes from Me.

Day 94

Treasures

Open your heart to My presence, unlock the door.
You have the power to either let Me in or shut Me
out. It is up to you. You need to open up, just like
you need to open your mouth to eat or drink. Your
heart is your inner life, and your heart is at your
command. Do not permit others to command your
heart. Not even I dare to control you. Guard your
heart. Guard what enters your heart. Shut out all
that is not of Me. I desire to give you much that will
build you up. I desire to fill your heart with the
things of heaven. I want you to be full of joy and
gladness so that your heart overflows with
thanksgiving.

*Offer to God a sacrifice of thanksgiving, and perform
your vows to the Most High, and call upon Me in the
day of trouble; I will deliver you, and you shall
glorify Me.*
Psalms 50:14-15 ESV

I pour My treasure into your heart and you store up
for yourself treasures in heaven. Continue to receive
My joy all throughout this day.

Attention

I love your attention. I love your openness to Me. I will not come unless you eagerly expect Me and long for what I have for you. It is as I showed My disciples when they traveled to a village. They should only stay if the peace they bid was received.

I identify with you because you are in Me. If people ignore you, they ignore Me. If people receive you, they receive Me. If people persecute you, they persecute Me. You have marveled at this. I want you to see other people like this. I want you to identify others with Me. As you love Me, so love them.

I manifest myself differently through various people. In one person I am a conqueror, pushing ahead through obstacles. In another person I am the deep wisdom of God and only those who dip into that well will find My gift. In yet another I am like a flowing river of joy. I can be a sword, a towel or a hug depending on the person. Are these not, as I showed Paul, just the different expressions of the Spirit as the various parts of the body? It is a wonder. Remember you are for signs and wonders. You, My people, not only do the signs and wonders, but you are the signs and wonders. What I do in you, unseen by you, manifests itself to the world and is a wonderful thing.

Day 96

Hooked up

You are hooked up with Me. I'm the engine, you are a passenger car. I pull, you go. Sometimes you think that you need to have all this drive, but I am already motivating and driving you. Relax about that part of your life. Don't struggle and fret and worry that you don't have what it takes. You have Me and that's all it takes. You've surrendered your will to Me, so here we go. Listen to Me and hear My voice. Be assured in My love and in My will. You have the mind of Christ, you do the will of Christ and you have the love of Christ flowing in and out of you. Your soul is being permeated with Me and the dark corners are being lit up. If on your path there are others who are not heading in the same direction you're going, you will be a light, but you don't have to fret about it. I have made you to be an example that others can see and follow, but you don't have to feel guilty if they don't.

If you are filled with light, with no dark corners, then your whole life will be radiant, as though a floodlight were filling you with light.
Luke 11:36 NLT

Surrendered Will

You are precious to me. I will show myself strong through you. Do not fear. I will give you abundant gifts of faith and you will know my power in your weakness. Be patient and don't worry about feeling exposed and vulnerable. I protect you. You needed this season of coming to the end of yourself. This will not be forever. Rest in me now, and draw near to me. Do not draw back.

Therefore do not cast away your confidence, which has great reward. For you have need of endurance, so that after you have done the will of God, you may receive the promise: 'For yet a little while and He who is coming will come and will not tarry. Now the just shall live by faith: But if anyone draws back, My soul has no pleasure in him.' But we are not of those who draw back to perdition, but of those who believe to the saving of the soul
Hebrews 10:35-39

Did I take it lightly when the widow offered her all to me? Did I look down at that and say, "All she has is two mites?" No, I made an example of her and I honored her. So I will honor you.

Day 98

Come

Come to me and you will find rest for your soul.
Come to me, open up to me. I'm here for you. I
know who you are. I know your needs. I have
created you. It doesn't come as a shock to me that
you need reassurance, love, affection and direction
daily. I put those needs into you for a reason. These
are the needs that keep you coming back to me.
These are the needs that keep you in sympathy to
others. Remember to come to me first so your cup
runs over.

You are seated with me in heavenly places. You are
already more honorable than you know. You are a
king and a priest with me. You are a chosen
generation, a royal priesthood, a holy nation, my
own special people, that you may proclaim my
praises because I called you out of darkness into my
marvelous light. You are in the light. You are
precious.

Come to me as your fortress, come to me as your
strength. Come to me as your Shepherd. Come to
me as my beloved. Come to me as my servant.
Come to me as my friend.

Breakthrough

I am the source of your joy and strength. Even if you receive from others, I am the source. No one can give you anything that matters unless it comes from Me. I am the only source of AGAPE love. I am the only source of ZOE life, and of DYNAMUS power. Without Me you can do nothing, but with Me all things are possible. As you seek me I will give you my will and my zeal and my life and my strength and my love. Do not look at what you lack. You lack no good thing. I put you precisely where I want you. Don't despise who you are. Appreciate your weakness for it allows me to be preeminent in you. Don't forget to come to me for affirmation each day. Why do you not come? Do you think you can love yourself more than I love you? Your love for yourself is so fickle, inconsistent and conditional. Come to my light. Come to my path. Come close to me where my love and grace will enable you to be more than you ever imagined. What if you lived in my joy at all times? What if you lived in my power? What if you lived in my favor? What if your mind would release doubt and insecurity and bitter judgment? When you come to me for affirmation each day, that's what will happen. Break through, break through, break through. There is yet more for you. There is yet greater victory, greater passion, greater connection to me. Break through, break through, break through. I am the Lord of the breakthrough.

Day 100

To the End of the Age

Since everything around us is going to melt away, what holy and godly lives you should live, looking forward to the day of God and hurrying it along. On that day, he will set the heavens on fire, and the elements will melt away in the flames. But we are looking forward to the new heavens and new earth he has promised, a world filled with God's righteousness.
2 Peter 3:11-13 NLT

I have given My children knowledge of the future. Who else knows what will happen and has an assurance of the safety I provide - None but My children. My Word is filled with glimpses of the days you live in. Yes, even now the will of God is unfolding and the seals are being opened in heaven. My children are not surprised by the evil in this world. Look forward to the glories to come, but now, be steadfast and lead holy and godly lives. While there is still time, do what I have commanded you to do:

Go therefore and make disciples of all nations, baptizing them in the name of the Father and of the Son and of the Holy Spirit, teaching them to observe all that I have commanded you. And behold, I am with you always, to the end of the age.
Matthew 28:19-20

LoveJoy PUBLISHING

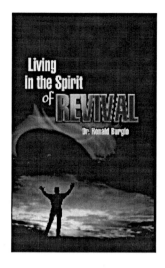

Living in the Spirit of Revival
by Dr. Ronald Burgio

Are you ready to live in the Spirit of Revival?

Would you like your church not only to experience revival, but also to maintain the Spirit of revival for years after the newness and freshness wears thin?

Are you ready to pay the price of revival? When opposition and persecution comes, will you and those around you stand firm? What do you expect of God in reviving you and other Christians around you?

Revival is for you and your church. Whether you are a pastor, leader, or believer hungry and desperate for God, this book is for you. It's time to experience the power and impact of revival in your life today!

LoveJoy PUBLISHING

Diana – Escape to Significance
A novel by Uta Milewski

Paperback $9.95
Call 716 651-0400 to order

Diana couldn't go back, not after what had happened. She would rather overcome the fear of the unknown, than to face again the fear of the known.

This sixteen year-old girl, abandoned by her father and orphaned by her mother, sought refuge with her stepsister in Iconium, a town in Phrygia in what we now know as Turkey.

Though her story plays in the 1st Century, many young women face the same questions in the 21st Century:

How can I make it through life? Can I find healing and freedom? Can I risk loving again and being loved?

CPSIA information can be obtained at www.ICGtesting.com
Printed in the USA
BVOW04s1354090514

352963BV00005B/51/P

9 780982 006214